Pts: 0.5

Elephants

Diane Swanson

Gareth Stevens Publishing
A WORLD ALMANAC EDUCATION GROUP COMPANY

Please visit our web site at: www.garethstevens.com
For a free color catalog describing Gareth Stevens Publishing's list of high-quality books
and multimedia programs, call 1-800-542-2595 (USA) or 1-800-387-3178 (Canada).
Gareth Stevens Publishing's fax: (414) 332-3567.

The publishers acknowledge the support of the Canada Council for the Arts and the Cultural Services
Branch of the Government of British Columbia in making this publication possible.

Library of Congress Cataloging-in-Publication Data

Swanson, Diane, 1944-
    Elephants / by Diane Swanson.
        p. cm. — (Welcome to the world of animals)
    Includes index.
    Summary: Describes the physical characteristics, behavior, habitat, and natural defenses
of the world's largest land animals, the African and Asian elephants, with emphasis on their
similarities and differences.
    ISBN 0-8368-4022-4 (lib. bdg.)
    1. Elephants—Juvenile literature. [1. Elephants.] I. Title.
QL737.P98S97   2004
599.67—dc22   2003059155

This edition first published in 2004 by
Gareth Stevens Publishing
A World Almanac Education Group Company
330 West Olive Street, Suite 100
Milwaukee, WI 53212 USA

This U.S. edition © 2004 by Gareth Stevens, Inc. Original edition © 2003 by Diane Swanson.
First published in 2003 by Whitecap Books, Vancouver, as *Welcome to the Whole World of Elephants*
in the *Welcome to the Whole World of Animals* series. Additional end matter © 2004
by Gareth Stevens, Inc.

Series editor: Betsy Rasmussen
Design: Melissa Valuch
Cover design: Steve Penner

Cover photograph: Thomas Kitchin
Photo credits: Thomas Kitchin 4, 12, 14, 20, 26; Wayne Lynch 6, 8, 10, 22; Wendy Dennis/
Dembinsky Photo Assoc. 16, 20; Anup Shah/Dembinsky Photo Assoc. 18, 28; Stan Osolinski/
Dembinsky Photo Assoc. 24

Printed in the United States of America

1 2 3 4 5 6 7 8 9 08 07 06 05 04

Contents

World of Difference

Elephants are enormous — the biggest land animals on Earth! African elephants are the tallest and heaviest elephants. Males grow up to 13 feet (4 meters) high at the shoulders and can weigh more than 7 tons (6 tonnes). Asian elephants are shorter and lighter than African elephants, but they are still huge animals.

Both kinds of elephants have long trunks. Trunks are used mostly for breathing, smelling, feeling, and grabbing things, such as food. At the end of its trunk, an African elephant has two fingerlike parts; an Asian elephant has one. These nimble

An African elephant has large ears.

Two bulges mark the forehead of an Asian elephant.

parts can pick up objects as small as berries.

Male and female African elephants have long pointed teeth, called tusks, that stick out of their mouths. The sharp tusks make good weapons for fighting, but more often they are used as tools for digging and scraping. Elephants usually favor either their right or their left tusk, just as people prefer using one hand more than the other. But most female and many male Asian elephants have no tusks at all.

Elephants see better in shadows than in bright light, but they depend more on their strong senses of smell and touch to explore their world. They hear quite well, too, and they use their big, floppy ears to help threaten their enemies. Held out to the sides, the ears make elephants look even larger than they already are.

EXTRAORDINARY ELEPHANTS

Here are some neat elephant facts.

- **Underwater, elephants can use their trunks like snorkels to breathe.**

- **Tusks never stop growing. One African elephant tusk measured about 11 feet (3.5 meters).**

- **A tall elephant may hold out one of its ears to shade a shorter elephant from the Sun.**

- **Elephants can find distant watering holes, even ones they haven't visited for months.**

Where in the World

Lush, green forests and dry, brown grasslands are homes for elephants. Some elephants live on cool, rugged mountains; others on hot, flat plains. But elephants seldom wander far from streams or lakes.

Each kind of elephant is named for the continent on which it is found. African elephants live in parts of Africa south of the Sahara Desert. Asian elephants live in parts of southern Asia, including India.

Wherever they roam, elephants need plenty of space. Because they are so big, they have to travel far and wide to find enough food. Adult males travel alone or,

An elephant grazes as it travels.

9

The shady jungle helps keep an elephant cool.

occasionally, with a few other males. But female elephants walk together. They move as families of sisters, daughters, aunts, and nieces — along with all their newborns and calves that are less than ten or twelve years old. A family group is usually led by its eldest female. She is also likely to be the largest in the family because elephants never stop growing.

When a family of elephants is on the move, it often meets other families. Then the families might travel together for a while as a herd.

Stopping for naps night and day, elephants search for sheltered sleeping places. They might lie down, sometimes gathering soft plants to form pillows beneath their heavy heads. But elephants frequently sleep standing up, resting their trunks on the ground.

ELEPHANTS ON ICE

Wild elephants today live in warm climates, but that wasn't always the case. Of the five hundred different kinds of elephants that have roamed Earth during the last several million years, some were well adapted to cold climates.

Ancient elephants called woolly mammoths even survived in North America and in the far north of Russia. Thick layers of fat and dense hairy coats kept them warm. The mammoths dug through snow with their curved tusks to reach grass.

11

World Full of Food

Eating is a full-time job for an elephant. To support its gigantic body, an elephant eats many meals every day. In just twenty-four hours, an adult elephant can eat food that weighs as much as eight hundred to thirteen hundred hamburgers!

During the wet seasons in Africa and Asia, elephants graze on grass, grabbing big bunches with their trunks. They might beat the grass against their front legs to shake dirt off the roots before eating. In the dry seasons, elephants eat from trees, using their trunks to pluck leaves and twigs. Sometimes an elephant stands only on

Standing tall, an elephant stretches to snatch leaves from a tree.

its back legs so its trunk can reach leaves that are high above ground.

Elephants also dine on fruit and seedpods, which they pick or shake from trees. They often wade into lakes and swamps to get to water plants. And elephants drink by sucking up water with their trunks. Then they tilt their heads back, stick the tips of their

With a bite of lunch curled tightly in its trunk, an elephant feeds.

14

trunks inside their mouths, and let the water flow.

Elephants use their trunks to put food into their mouths. In one minute, they can gather and eat nine or ten trunkfuls of grass. Four huge teeth — each one longer than this page — grind up every bite.

An elephant's teeth wear down or fall out and are replaced several times during an elephant's life. When the last set of teeth is completely worn down—usually in fifty to seventy years—the elephant can no longer chew, and it will die.

UNDERGROUND ELEPHANTS

Just like people, elephants need a little salt in their diets. Along the border between Kenya and Uganda, African elephants file into a mountain cave to "mine" for salt.

The elephants use their trunks to feel their way through the deep, dark cave. When they find some salt rocks, they chip them out with their tusks. The animals visit the cave almost nightly, earning the nickname "underground elephants."

World of Words

Elephants use their trunks to communicate. A calf hooks its trunk around its mother's back leg to say, "Wait!" An adult slaps its trunk on a calf to say it is time to settle down. Trunks are also used to hug and pat family members. The animals might flap their ears as well, which strengthens the message: "I like you."

Like many other animals, elephants communicate through sounds, too. They trumpet loudly with their trunks, announcing that they are angry or excited. Young calves growl to let their mothers know they are hungry, and they scream

One elephant pats another in a friendly "hello."

17

A calf lets its mother know that it is ready for another meal.

to demand attention. Adults sometimes bark at older calves, warning them not to wander off.

But a lot of elephant talk cannot be heard by people. Many of the animals' sounds are too low-pitched to be picked up by human ears. Trees and grasses do not block these low rumblings as much as they do high-pitched sounds, such as whistles. That means elephants can send low-pitched messages to other elephants more than 2.5 miles (4 kilometers) away. These messages also make the ground vibrate, which sends the signals even farther.

All this long-distance communication is important for animals that travel around as much as elephants do. It helps males and females find one another when they are ready to mate. And it might warn families of danger or tell them the locations of watering holes.

FOLLOWING ORDERS

Elephants not only understand each other, they can also learn to understand people. Human trainers teach the animals to follow about one hundred different commands, such as kneel, stand, go, turn, stop, and lift. The elephants can also learn new skills, including untying knots and sitting down — something they do not do naturally.

Trained elephants are used to carry people, entertain crowds, and do heavy work, such as lifting and hauling logs.

New World

When they are only an hour old, elephants can walk and even keep up with their family. But the newborns move stiffly and trip easily. They often step on their own trunks and fall down. Then they cry—noisy, squeaky screams—for attention.

It does not take a young elephant long to start exploring. From its first day, a newborn uses its trunk to smell, feel, and tug whatever is around. Soon it tries to lift things, too. But sometimes the little calf takes time out to suck the tip of its trunk, much like a human baby sucks a thumb.

When there's nothing much to do, a calf can always suck its trunk.

Asian elephants watch protectively over a young calf.

A calf spends most of its first few months close to its mother. She pats and strokes the calf as it leans against her. Frequently, the calf stays right beneath her belly as they walk. And when they nap, a baby usually lays its head on its mother's body.

At first, the calf feeds only on its

mother's milk, but soon it starts nibbling grass and leaves as well. It also learns to drink water, kneeling at first to sip with its mouth before trying to draw the water up its trunk.

Mother elephants get help raising their calves. Other females and older calves keep a close eye on a newborn. They try to make sure it does not wander off, but if it does, they are quick to bring it back.

Lions in Africa and tigers in Asia might attack a young elephant. If they threaten a calf, the older elephants in the family form a protective circle around the calf.

HELP FROM GRANDMA

Being born into a family with an old leader helps an elephant calf grow strong and stay safe. An old elephant can draw on many memories of searching for food and water. And she can usually find the best places for her family to eat and drink.

The older elephant also remembers the calls of many of the elephants she meets, so she can sort friends from strangers. Then the family can act to protect its calves from unfriendly elephants.

Small World

Elephant calves have a lot to learn. Even eating takes practice. One of the hardest skills a calf has to master is feeding on short grass. The calf tries to wind its trunk around a single blade of grass—something that calls for several patient attempts. When the calf breaks off the blade, it is likely to drop the grass. Then the elephant struggles, again and again, to pick it up.

When hunger makes a calf too impatient to try to feed with its trunk, it might drop down on its knees and simply bite off the grass. Or it might snatch bits of food as they fall from the mouths of bigger

Sneaking close, a calf steals food from an older elephant's mouth.

Ah! There is nothing like a mud bath to make a calf feel like playing.

elephants. Some calves try to yank grass and leaves right out of the munching mouths of others.

Calves must learn to groom themselves. They shower and bathe, rolling around in shallow water. Then they use their trunks to suck up dust or mud and spray their bodies. This layer of dirt helps get rid of pests and protects the elephants from the strong Sun.

A calf soon discovers it can relieve itches by scratching with the tip of its trunk or by rubbing itself against trees. For hard-to-reach places, such as the belly, it figures out how to hold a stick with its trunk and scratch.

As a calf gets older, its mother lets other family members answer its cries more and more often. Then she has time to look after herself and, perhaps, a new calf. Elephants are often born four years apart.

THICK AND WRINKLY

As a young elephant matures, its skin grows thicker. Parts of its hide become four times as thick as human skin. Still, the hide is sensitive. Elephants, like people, can sunburn and sense insect bites.

Having wrinkled skin is good for an elephant. The deep creases hold moisture, which cools the animal. The wrinkles also help make each elephant different. The pattern of wrinkles on its lower legs are unique in each individual elephant.

Fun World

Big elephants and little elephants—all elephants play. And when elephants of different sizes play together, the taller ones make themselves "shorter" by kneeling or lying down.

Elephant calves spend the greatest amount of time at play. One of their favorite games is climbing on large elephants that are lying on the grass. The calves also stretch out together, especially wherever there is mud. Then they scramble and slide over one another's slippery bodies.

Many elephant games involve running. One animal might chase after another and

Two playmates take part in an elephant game.

29

Young elephants enjoy some clean, wet fun together.

try to grab it by the tail. Or two elephants might pretend to charge. They trumpet loudly and gallop toward each other. Sometimes elephants butt heads or pretend to fight by pushing and shoving or by wrestling with their trunks.

Water play is fun for elephants. They like to splash and make waves. Best of all, they suck water up their trunks and spray it at their playmates.

Elephant toys are whatever elephants can find. Calves toss leaves into the air, then dash through them. Adults fling small trees. Elephants even attack logs, stomping and kicking them until they break.

With their families close by for safety, young calves might spend only ten minutes playing before they get tired. But the games of older calves and adult elephants can last for more than an hour.

BUFFALO PLAYMATES

A male elephant calf on an African plain is hiding in tall grass. Only a few months old, he is ready and eager for fun. Usually he plays with other elephants in his family. But today, he cannot resist teasing cape buffalo calves.

As a herd of cape buffalo wanders by, the little elephant suddenly bursts out of the grass, startling one of the calves. Then he returns to his hiding spot until the next calf appears, and he charges out again.

Glossary

climates — area weather conditions.

continent — one of the seven major land masses of the world. North America is one of Earth's continents.

dense — packed together tightly.

hide — a heavy skin covering of an animal.

high-pitched — sounds that have a piercing or shrill quality.

low-pitched — sounds that have a deep quality.

snorkels — devices that stick above the water, allowing a swimmer to breathe when underwater.

trumpet — to make a sound that resembles that of a musical instrument called a trumpet.

tusks — long teeth that stick out of the mouth when the mouth is closed. They are used for digging or fighting.

woolly mammoths — extinct ancestors of elephants. They had heavy coats of hair on their hides.

Index